Smoothie Recipes for Rapid Weight Loss

50 Delicious, Quick & Easy Recipes to Help Melt Your Damn Stubborn Fat Away!

Disclaimer

This document is geared towards providing exact and reliable information in regards to the topic and issue covered. The publication is sold with the idea that the publisher is not required to render accounting, officially permitted, or otherwise, qualified services. If advice is necessary, legal or professional, a practiced individual in the profession should be ordered.

- From a Declaration of Principles which was accepted and approved equally by a Committee of the American Bar Association and a Committee of Publishers and Associations.

About This Book

This book aims to introduce you to the benefits of smoothies and give you 50 of the best smoothie recipes for rapid weight loss. It's informational and to the point, and organized into sections on non-dairy green smoothies and dairy-based smoothies so you won't be missing anything. Each section is complete with the needed information.

You will find concluding remarks and a list of resources for additional recipes at the end of this book. I will also give you a preview of another book of mine which I am sure will delight you as well.

The following table of contents will show you exactly what is covered in this book.

Table of Contents

Introduction

I probably don't need to tell you how hard it is to lose weight. Yes, I know about the TV ads that tell us about how easy it is. I've seen the latest diet pills, exercise machines and fad diets that supposedly miraculously shed X number of pounds instantly. But those of us who've tried these "quick solutions" know that, while these miraculous fads might help you take off a few pounds quickly, those pounds are probably going to return just as quickly.

To get long-term results, you need to find fundamental, long-term solutions. You need to make basic changes in your lifestyle that keep you feeling energetic and satisfied so that you won't have the cravings that lead to binging. You need a low-calorie diet that doesn't leave you feeling so drained that you eventually have to resort to eating sugary or fatty foods just to keep your energy up.

Green smoothies can supercharge your system with nutrients that provide you with an abundance of energy. This increased energy will lead to an increase in your activity level, which will in turn increase your metabolic rate. This, in turn, will start burning up the stubborn fat you've been trying to shed.

A well-made smoothie tastes great and leaves you feeling satisfied, acting as an appetite suppressant while reducing your caloric intake. Making smoothies is an easy way to make a permanent lifestyle change that can leave you feeling healthier, happier and trimmer.

This book provides you with fifty simple recipes for delicious smoothies that take only a few minutes to make. The book also provides you with the info you need to design your own recipes according to your own needs and tastes.

I hope you're able to put this book to good use. Thanks for downloading it.

Tips for Making Smoothies

Here are some tips for making smoothing. The first section is for general tips and the second section is for creating your own recipes.

General Tips

Use ripe fruit. Unripe fruit isn't very sweet, so it doesn't do a good job of sweetening up your bitter greens. Unripe fruit is harder to digest than ripe fruit and isn't as healthful.

Blend leafy vegetables first. Leafy vegetables are often hard to blend when they're mixed in with fruit. By blending the leafy vegetables first, along with the liquid base (milk, juice, tea or water), you avoid this problem. Chopping the leaves up beforehand can also help.

Try using frozen fruits and leafy vegetables. As an alternative to using ice in a smoothie, you can use one or two frozen vegetables or fruits, putting them directly into the blender without thawing them. Freezing your fruits and vegetables is also a good way to keep them from getting overly ripe.

If your schedule is loaded, make your smoothie ahead of time. If you have a busy schedule, you can make your smoothie the night before and store it in an airtight container in the fridge. This eliminates the need for putting ice cubes or frozen fruit in your smoothie. It also ensures that the smoothie is evenly cool throughout. You can store smoothies for up to two days in a fridge.

Prep your smoothies. Another way to help with your scheduling is to prep your smoothies ahead of time, putting the ingredients for each smoothie recipe into a plastic bag and putting that into the fridge. You can do this for a week or more in advance. This also helps with grocery shopping, because you'll know ahead of time what you're running out of.

Change things up. Variety is the spice of life. Drinking the same smoothies day after day can not only get boring but can limit the nutrients you're putting into your body. So mix it up a bit. You can also make small substitutions in recipes, changing up your choice of vegetables and fruits. You can also substitute the type of liquid base in a recipe, using orange juice, apple juice, cashew milk, almond milk, coconut water or coconut milk in place of plain water or whatever else the recipe calls for. But be sparing at first in your substitutions, or you might end up with a train wreck.

Investigate superfoods. If you want to add variety and nutrition to your smoothies, you might check out certain so-called "superfoods" like acai powder, maca powder, cacao powder, goji berries, spirulina, yacon, lucuma powder, bee pollen and coconut palm sugar. These items tend to be pricey, but most of them pack a wallop, and you only have to add a small amount to your smoothie. You should experiment with very small amounts at first, because some of them will add wild flavors or colors.

Consider putting thick smoothies into a bowl. If you've made an extra thick smoothie or you want to add granola, nuts or other toppings to it, you might try putting the smoothie into a bowl and eating it with a spoon.

Tips for Creating Your Own Recipes

Stick with the tried-and-true recipes at first. Don't start making up your own recipes until you've sampled a wide variety of green smoothies; this affords you the opportunity to get a good idea of what you like and dislike in smoothies before you take the leap into creating your own recipes. This also allows you to develop a taste for certain ingredients you might not be used to.

Start with mild greens. Certain vegetables like kale and parsley have a strong taste that can overpower everything else in a smoothie, so you should start off by using mild greens like spinach. Then you can start mixing mild greens with stronger vegies, gradually increasing the amounts of the stronger ones.

Use at least one sweet fruit. To counteract the bitterness or strong flavors of vegetables like kale, you'll need to add at least one sweet fruit, such as apples, oranges, peaches, mangos, dates, raisins, berries, etc. If you concoct a smoothie that doesn't taste right, adding a sweet fruit will often fix the problem. Sweet fruits can also provide an energy boost on an active day. However, sweet fruits normally have quite a few calories, and they can spike your blood sugar levels.

Watch your ratios. When making up a recipe, you should try to stay as close as possible to the proper ratio of fruit/greens/liquid, at least at first. What is the proper ratio? That's open to debate, but a general rule of thumb is to include one cup of green vegetables, one-and-a-half cups of fruit and one cup of base liquid per recipe. This basically yields one serving. You can use less fruit and more greens if the fruit or the liquid base is sweet. If you're using strong-flavored greens, you'll need to include more sweet fruit or some type of added sweetener. As you get more used to green smoothies, your tastes might change, perhaps allowing you to cut back on the amount of sweets.

Try a carrot juice base. If you want to maximize your vegetables and minimize your fruit, you can use a carrot juice base, which is fairly sweet and quite nutritious.

Try including something creamy. Including creamy fruits like bananas, avocados, pears and peaches will render a nice, creamy texture to a smoothie. Peanut butter, almond butter and other nut butters are terrific for this, too, though you'll want to use them in small amounts because of their calories.

For aesthetics, use light-colored ingredients. If you're making a smoothie for guests, you might want to avoid using many dark-colored ingredients like blueberries that might turn your green smoothie into something that resembles brown sludge.

Superstar Smoothie Ingredients

Greens

Leafy greens are high in chlorophyll, antioxidants and many other nutrients, while being low in calories.

Spinach

Because it has a delicate flavor that is easily masked by other flavors, spinach is the most popular green for smoothies, particularly for newbies. Some people consider spinach a superfood because it's a good source of fiber, lutein, antioxidants, calcium, iron and vitamins A, C, K and folate. It also contains selenium, zinc, phosphorus, copper, omega-3 fatty acids and vitamins B1, B2, B3, B6 and E. The one drawback of spinach is that it's high in oxalic acid, so if you're prone to kidney stones, you should limit your use of spinach.

Chard

Because of its delicate flavor, chard—like its cousin spinach—is a good choice for smoothies. Its soft leaves blend easily in any blender. Chard is an excellent source of vitamins A and K, and is also a good source of protein and vitamins C and E. It's also a good source of copper, manganese, magnesium and natural sodium. Unfortunately, like spinach, chard is high in oxalic acid.

Kale

Kale is a very good source of beta carotene, vitamins C and K, lutein, calcium and fiber, and is a fairly good source of many other nutrients. It contains sulforaphane, which is supposedly an excellent cancer fighter. It also has been shown to promote healthy lungs, boost the immune system and fight inflammation. Kale has a strong flavor, so it's usually accompanied in recipes by strong-flavored ingredients that mask its flavor, like strawberries or pineapple.

Collards

Collards have a fairly mild but slightly bitter taste. They're a great source of Vitamin K and fiber, and a good source of Vitamin A, lutein and protein. They also contain a fair amount of calcium and iron. Collards are less bitter than their cousins, kale and dandelion.

Dandelion

Dandelion greens are loaded with calcium, iron and Vitamin A, and are a fairly good source of numerous other nutrients. They also have numerous medicinal properties and are considered to reduce the risk of cancer, multiple sclerosis cataracts, macular degeneration, asthma, inflammatory diseases and stroke. They're quite bitter tasting, but what medicine isn't?

Avocados

Avocados are technically a fruit, but in smoothies they function more like a non-leafy vegetable. Because they're somewhat of a hybrid vegetable/fruit, they have a mild flavor that combines well with just about any fruit or vegetable. Avocados are excellent for creating a creamy consistency in smoothies, and they add healthy fats that fill you up and satisfy your hunger.

Fruits

Fruits provide a quick energy burst and a lot of nutrients. They also mask the flavor of raw greens that might otherwise render a smoothie unpalatable.

Berries

Strawberries, blackberries, blueberries and raspberries add a lot of fiber, antioxidants and flavor to smoothies without adding a lot of sugar or calories. They're also among the highest foods in ellagic acid, a substance that might help fight cancer.

Apples

Apples add bulk and sweetness to a smoothie without adding a lot of calories, making you feel fuller without adding much fat. Apples combine well with many other ingredients, helping to mask the flavor of bitter ingredients without overpowering a smoothie with sweetness. Strangely, apples have been shown to help regulate blood sugar levels, actually helping to prevent spikes in your blood sugar. Apples are a fairly good source of fiber, and they've been shown to provide many of the same fat-lowering benefits that are normally associated with foods that possess a much higher level of fiber. Apples also help reduce cholesterol and can help in fighting cancer, asthma, Alzheimer's and other ailments.

Bananas

Bananas provide some nutritional benefits, but their main value is in their ability to provide a deliciously creamy texture to smoothies. Bananas also provide a mellow sweetness that blends well with most other smoothie ingredients.

Citrus

Oranges, limes, lemons and grapefruit are great sources of vitamin C and cancer-fighting flavonoids and are good sources of many other nutrients. They help prevent blood clots and also help cleanse your body of toxins. They're also useful in providing a sweet liquid base for smoothies.

Other Stars

Chia Seeds

Chia seeds are packed with fiber and protein, so they help you feel full and satisfied. They contain good amounts of calcium, antioxidants and omega-3 fatty acids, and they absorb toxins from your digestive tract. They also add creaminess to the texture of smoothies.

Cayenne Pepper

Cayenne adds a kick to smoothies without adding many calories, and it can aid your digestion. It also serves as a powerful appetite suppressant, a valuable tool for weight-watchers.

Cinnamon

Cinnamon not only adds a nice flavor but also helps to regulate blood sugar levels in your body. It improves the metabolism of glucose, limiting the amount of glucose that can be stored in your body as fat, thus saving you some poundage.

Green Tea

Green tea is a low-calorie substitute for fruit juice bases. Green tea provides some nutrients, including a compound that apparently aids in weight loss.

Coconut Oil

Coconut oil is also almost an anti-fat, as the predominant fats it contains are used to provide energy instead of being stored as fat. Coconut oil makes you feel full, serving as an appetite suppressant. Coconut oil also increases your good cholesterol levels while decreasing your bad.

Dairy-free Green Smoothies

Note: The numbers after the recipes refer to our sources for the recipes. See the Helpful Resources section toward the end of the book.

Kale Banana Soy (1)

The banana taste hides the kale from your kids, so they won't know how nutritious this delicious recipe is.

Serves 1.

Ingredients

- 1 banana
- 2 cups chopped kale
- ½ cup light unsweetened soy milk
- 1 tablespoon flax seeds
- 1 teaspoon maple syrup

Directions

1. Thoroughly wash the kale.

2. Blend the soy milk and kale in a blender until smooth. Add the rest of the ingredients and blend them until smooth.

3. Serve.

Green Slime (1)

Kids go for this one because of the name.

Makes 4 cups.

Ingredients

- 2 cups spinach, frozen for one hour
- 2 cups frozen strawberries
- 1 banana
- 2 tablespoons honey
- ½ cup ice

Directions

1. Thoroughly wash the strawberries and spinach.

2. Put all the ingredients into a blender and blend them until smooth.

3. Serve immediately.

Dr. Oz's Green Drink (3)

A high-fiber way to jumpstart your morning.

Serves 3.

Ingredients

- 2 cups spinach
- ½ cucumber
- ¼ head celery
- ½ bunch parsley
- 1 bunch mint
- 3 carrots
- 2 apples, cored
- ¼ orange
- ¼ lime
- ¼ lemon
- ¼ pineapple

Directions

1. Thoroughly wash the fruits and vegetables.

2. Put all the ingredients into a blender and blend them until smooth.

3. Serve.

Cilantro Pineapple Avocado (6)

This smoothie is rich in nutrients and is a good cleanser.

Serves 1.

Ingredients

- 1 ½ cups fresh spinach
- ½ cup fresh cilantro
- 2 cups water
- 1 ½ cups mango
- 1 cup pineapple
- ½ cup avocado

Directions

- Thoroughly wash the applicable fruits and vegetables.

- Blend the spinach, cilantro and water until smooth. Add everything else and blend until smooth.

- Serve.

Banana Spinach Berry (6)

You can substitute a navel orange for the orange juice. You can also add a few drops of Echinacea, olive leaf extract or elderberry extract, each of which helps boost your immune system.

Serves 1.

Ingredients

- 2 cups fresh spinach
- ¾ cup water
- ¾ cup orange juice
- 1 cup strawberries
- 1 cup blueberries
- 2 bananas

Directions

- Thoroughly wash the applicable fruits and vegetables.

- Blend the spinach, orange juice and water until smooth. Add everything else and blend until smooth. If you want a cold smoothie, either substitute ice for the water or freeze at least one of the other ingredients.

- Serve.

Pomegranate Spinach Banana (6)

Boosts your immune system and adds antioxidants.

Serves 1.

Ingredients

- 2 cups fresh spinach
- 1 cup orange juice, fresh squeezed
- 1 cup water
- 1 cup pomegranate seeds
- 1 banana

Directions

1. Thoroughly wash the applicable fruits and vegetables.

2. Blend the spinach, orange juice and water until smooth. Add everything else and blend until smooth. If you want a cold smoothie, either substitute ice for the water or freeze at least one of the other ingredients.

3. Serve.

Kale Strawberry Kiwi (6)

You can sub nearly any green for the dandelion.

Serves 1.

Ingredients

- 1 cup fresh kale greens
- 1 cup fresh dandelion greens
- 2 cups fresh orange juice
- 2 cups strawberries
- 2 kiwis (peeled or unpeeled)
- 1 banana
- 1 squeezed lemon

Directions

1. Thoroughly wash the applicable fruits and vegetables.

2. Blend the kale, dandelion and orange juice until smooth. Add the other ingredients and blend until smooth.

3. You can optionally add ice or freeze one of the ingredients to make the drink cold.

4. Serve.

Kale Banana Avocado (6)

Deliciously creamy.

Serves 1.

Ingredients

- 2 cups fresh kale
- 2 cups water
- ¼ avocado
- 3 bananas

Directions

1. Thoroughly wash the applicable fruits and vegetables.

2. Blend the kale and water until smooth. Add everything else and blend until smooth. If you want a cold smoothie, either substitute ice for the water or freeze at least one of the other ingredients.

3. Serve.

Coconut Collards Oats (7)

Collards are a neglected and underrated food, being nutritionally similar to spinach. This smoothie offers a rich and filling treat when you want to splurge a little or reward yourself after a good workout.

Serves 2.

Ingredients

- ½ cup coconut milk
- 1 cup green collards
- ¼ cup rolled oats
- 2 tablespoons sliced almonds
- 2 cups almond milk
- 2 tablespoons honey
- 4 ice cubes

Directions

1. Thoroughly wash the applicable fruits and vegetables.

2. Put all the ingredients into a blender and blend them until smooth.

3. Serve.

Spinach Pineapple Banana (9)

This is a popular recipe because of its mild yet fairly sweet flavor.

Serves 2.

Ingredients

- 2 cups fresh spinach
- 2 cups water
- 1 cup mango
- 1 cup pineapple
- 2 bananas

Directions

1. Thoroughly wash the applicable fruits and vegetables.

2. Blend the spinach and water until smooth. Add everything else and blend until smooth.

3. If you want a cold smoothie, either substitute ice for the water or freeze at least one of the other ingredients.

4. Serve.

Coconut Kale Orange (10)

Kale and oranges are simply loaded with natural fiber, so this is a good recipe for cleansing. Kale has a strong flavor that some people take a while to get used to, so you might want to start out with curly kale, which has a milder flavor.

Serves 2.

Ingredients

- 1 banana, peeled
- 1 orange, peeled and deseeded
- 1 medium carrot, chopped
- 3 cups curly kale leaves
- 8 ounces unsweetened coconut milk

Directions

1. Thoroughly wash the applicable fruits and vegetables.

2. Blend the kale and milk until smooth. Add everything else and blend until smooth. Serve.

Celery Strawberries Oats (10)

With ingredients like celery, beets and oats, this isn't exactly your typical green smoothie. But those ingredients blend wonderfully here with strawberries and coconut water for a treat that is rich in nutrients.

Serves 2.

Ingredients

- ½ cup beet root, chopped
- ¼ avocado, peeled and pitted
- 1 stalk celery
- 10 strawberries, fresh or frozen
- ¼ cup dry old fashioned oats
- 8 ounces (236 ml) coconut water

Directions

1. Thoroughly wash the applicable fruits and vegetables.

2. Blend all the ingredients until smooth.

3. Serve.

Dandelion Honeydew Cucumber (10)

Dandelions are an excellent source of protein, fiber and minerals (particularly calcium and iron), and are also high in vitamins A and C.

Serves 1.

Ingredients

- 3 cups dandelion greens
- ½ unpeeled cucumber
- 6 fresh mint leaves
- 8 ounces unsweetened almond milk
- 2 cups honeydew melon, cubed
- 1 frozen banana, sliced
- 1 teaspoon lime juice

Directions

1. Thoroughly wash the applicable fruits and vegetables.

2. Blend the dandelion, cucumber, mint and almond milk until smooth. Add everything else and blend until smooth.

3. Serve.

Collard Pomegranate Orange (10)

To get the seeds out of a pomegranate, cut the pomegranate in half and hold one of the halves (with the cut side down) over a bowl. Whack the skin all over, including the edges. The arils—which are the seeds and the juice pods that surround them—will fall out of the fruit. These arils are what you'll use in the smoothie. Normally, a medium-sized pomegranate will supply about a cup of arils.

Serves 1.

Ingredients

- 3 large collard leaves, stems removed
- 1 Bartlett pear, cored
- 2 oranges, peeled and deseeded
- ½ cup pomegranate arils
- 2 ounces water, if needed

Directions

1. Thoroughly wash the applicable fruits and vegetables.

2. Blend all the ingredients (except the water) until smooth. If necessary, add the water.

3. Serve.

Pear Raspberry Beet Oat (10)

The earthy flavor of the beet root is somewhat masked by the sweetness of the pear and raspberry.

Serves 1.

Ingredients

- ½ cup beet root, chopped
- 1 Bartlett pear, cored
- ¼ cup dry old fashion oats
- ½ cup fresh or frozen raspberries
- 2 cups fresh baby spinach
- 8 ounces water

Directions

1. Thoroughly wash the applicable fruits and vegetables.

2. Blend all the ingredients until smooth.

3. Serve.

Broccoli Banana Kale (10)

This might seem like a weird combo, with kale and peanut butter, but it's delicious. A little higher in calories than many of the other recipes, but it's a nice change of pace.

Serves 1.

Ingredients

- 1 cup baby kale
- 8 ounces water
- 2 small bananas
- 1 cup frozen broccoli
- 2 small bananas, peeled

Directions

1. Thoroughly wash the applicable fruits and vegetables.

2. Blend the kale and water until smooth. Add everything else and blend until smooth.

3. Serve.

Apple Banana Flax (11)

This calls for dandelion greens, but you can use spinach greens instead.

Serves 1.

Ingredients

- 1 bunch dandelion greens
- 8 ounces water
- 1 lemon, peeled
- 2 large apples
- 1 banana
- 2 teaspoons flax seeds

Directions

1. Thoroughly wash the applicable fruits and vegetables.

2. Blend the dandelion and water until smooth. Add everything else and blend until smooth.

3. Serve.

Carrot Ginger Avocado (11)

If you're brave, you can add some of the greens from the carrots to the mix.

Serves 1.

Ingredients

- 2 medium carrots
- 1 avocado
- ½ lemon, peeled
- ½ inch fresh ginger
- Pinch of sea salt
- Pinch of cayenne pepper
- 8 ounces water

Directions

1. Thoroughly wash the applicable fruits and vegetables.

2. Blend all the ingredients until smooth.

3. Serve.

Cilantro Banana Lime (12)

An interesting flavor combination.

Serves 2.

Ingredients

- ½ cup fresh cilantro
- 1 ½ cups fresh spinach
- 3 bananas
- 1 lime, peeled
- 1 inch fresh ginger
- 2 cups water

Directions

1. Thoroughly wash the applicable fruits and vegetables.

2. Blend the cilantro, spinach and water until smooth. Add everything else and blend until smooth.

3. Serve.

Kale Avocado Ginger (13)

Kale is loaded with antioxidants and other nutrients, and its strong taste is mellowed here by the avocado.

Serves 1.

Ingredients

- 1 cup kale
- 1 cup water
- 4 ice cubes
- ½ lemon, peeled and deseeded
- ½ lime, peeled
- ½ tablespoon ginger, peeled and grated
- ½ avocado
- Pinch salt

Directions

1. Thoroughly wash the applicable fruits and vegetables.

2. Blend the kale and water until smooth. Add everything else and blend until smooth.

3. Serve.

Cucumber Apple Nutmeg (13)

Nutmeg is known as a cellulite buster.

Serves 1.

Ingredients

- Handful of spinach
- 1 cup water
- 4 cubes ice
- 1 small cucumber, cut into chunks
- 1 apple, cored
- ½ lime, peeled
- ½ lemon, peeled
- 1/8 teaspoon nutmeg

Directions

1. Thoroughly wash the applicable fruits and vegetables.

2. Blend the spinach and water until smooth. Add everything else and blend until smooth.

3. Serve.

Spinach Berries Almond (14)

You can buy almond milk with no added sugar, which is better for your health and your waistline.

Serves 1.

Ingredients

- 1 cup almond milk
- 1 cup mixed berries (strawberry, blackberry, blueberry)
- ½ cup spinach leaves
- 1 scoop whey protein
- 1 tablespoon chia seeds

Directions

1. Thoroughly wash the applicable fruits and vegetables.

2. Blend the kale and water until smooth. Add everything else and blend until smooth. If you want a cold smoothie, freeze the berries or spinach beforehand.

3. Serve.

Kale Pineapple Mango (14)

Kale and spinach are among the most nutritionally rich foods on earth.

Serves 1.

Ingredients

- 1 cup coconut milk
- ¼ cup spinach
- ¼ cup kale
- ¼ cup frozen pineapple
- ¼ cup frozen mango

Directions

1. Thoroughly wash the applicable fruits and vegetables.

2. Blend the kale, spinach and coconut milk until smooth. Add everything else and blend until smooth.

3. Serve.

Kale Spinach Apple (14)

Kale, avocado and spinach are good for alkalizing your system.

Serves 1.

Ingredients

- 1 cup almond milk
- ¼ cup kale
- ¼ cup spinach
- ½ avocado
- 1 apple, cored
- 1 tablespoon honey

Directions

1. Thoroughly wash the applicable fruits and vegetables.

2. Blend the kale, spinach and almond milk until smooth. Add everything else and blend until smooth.

3. Serve.

Carrot Mango Strawberry (14)

As a twist, this recipe uses carrot juice as it only "green" vegetable.

Serves 1.

Ingredients

- 1 cup carrot juice
- ¼ cup frozen mango
- ½ frozen banana
- ¼ cup frozen pineapple
- ¼ cup strawberries

Directions

1. Thoroughly wash the applicable fruits and vegetables.

2. Blend all the ingredients until smooth.

3. Serve.

Cucumber Green Tea (14)

Green tea is said to help stimulate weight loss.

Serves 1.

Ingredients

- 1 cup green tea
- ½ cucumber
- 1 squeezed lime
- 5 ice cubes

Directions

1. Thoroughly wash the applicable fruits and vegetables.

2. Blend all the ingredients until smooth.

3. Serve.

Avocado Carrot Apple (14)

A deliciously mild flavor with a touch of sweetness.

Serves 1.

Ingredients

- 1 cup almond milk
- ½ avocado
- 1 apple, cored
- 5 baby carrots
- 5 ice cubes

Directions

1. Thoroughly wash the applicable fruits and vegetables.

2. Blend all the ingredients until smooth.

3. Serve.

Kale Mango Banana (15)

For a chunky variation, you can just cut the mango into chunks and add them to the mix after everything else has been blended.

Serves 1.

Ingredients

- 3 cups chopped kale leaves
- 1 whole medium-sized mango, cut into chunks
- ½ cup sliced banana
- ½ lime fruit
- 1 cup unsweetened coconut milk

Directions

1. Thoroughly wash the applicable fruits and vegetables.

2. Blend the kale and coconut until smooth. Add everything else and blend until smooth.

3. Serve.

Lettuce Pear Banana (15)

This mild-flavored smoothie is a safe choice to serve anyone at any time, and is a good choice for serving someone who's never tried a green smoothie. This is a light meal for one person or a snack for two.

Serves 2.

Ingredients

- 3 cups chopped romaine lettuce (about 1 head)
- 2 cups chopped spinach leaves
- ½ cup sliced celery
- 1 cup water
- ½ cup diced apples
- ¼ cup diced pear
- ½ cup sliced banana
- ½ tablespoon fresh lemon juice

Directions

1. Thoroughly wash the applicable fruits and vegetables.

2. Blend the lettuce, spinach, celery and water until smooth. Add everything else and blend until smooth.

3. Serve.

Collard Pineapple Orange (15)

This smoothie is packed with vitamins A, C, E and K, as well as numerous minerals.

Serves 1.

Ingredients

- 1 cup fresh spinach
- 1 cup fresh collard greens
- 4 whole medium sized oranges, squeezed
- 3 cups pineapple chunks
- 4 ice cubes (optional)

Directions

1. Thoroughly wash the applicable fruits and vegetables.

2. Blend all the ingredients until smooth.

3. Serve.

Spinach Papaya Mint (15)

If you want a creamier smoothie, you can substitute banana for the papaya.

Serves 1.

Ingredients

- 1 cup filtered water
- 3 cups spinach leaves
- 2 cups cubed ripe papaya
- 1 cup cubed pear
- 2 tablespoons goji berries (dried or fresh)
- 10 fresh leaves of mint

Directions

1. Thoroughly wash the applicable fruits and vegetables.

2. Blend the spinach and water until smooth. Add everything else and blend until smooth.

3. Serve.

Dandelion Pineapple Date (15)

You can add 3 tablespoons or raw, chopped walnuts or cashews as an added treat. Pre-soaking the nuts makes them easier to digest.

Serves 4.

Ingredients

- 1 cup chopped dandelion greens
- 2 cups unsweetened coconut water
- 4 cups fresh ripe pineapple chunks
- ½ cup shredded coconut meat
- 4 tablespoons dried pitted dates
- 2 cups ice cubes

Directions

1. Thoroughly wash the applicable fruits and vegetables.

2. Blend the dandelion and coconut water until smooth. Add everything else and blend until smooth.

3. Serve.

Romaine Chard Kiwi (15)

You can substitute papaya or mango for the kiwi. The bee pollen and maca powder are loaded with nutrients. However, if you've never tried bee pollen, eat three or four different-colored grains to test for an allergic reaction and then wait a few hours before taking any more. Maca powder is high in potassium, iodine and calcium, and contains many essential trace elements and amino acids.

Serves 1.

Ingredients

- 1 cup chopped kale leaves
- 1 cup chopped Romaine lettuce
- 1 cup chopped Swiss chard leaves
- 1 cup distilled water
- ½ cup sliced ripe bananas
- ½ kiwi fruit
- Juice of ½ lemon
- 1 teaspoon bee pollen
- ½ teaspoon maca powder

Directions

1. Thoroughly wash the applicable fruits and vegetables.

2. Blend the kale, lettuce, chard and water until smooth. Add everything else and blend until smooth.

3. Serve.

Cashew Date Mint (15)

Mint triggers a feeling of fullness, serving as an appetite suppressant. It also aids in digestion.

Serves 2.

Ingredients

- 1 ½ cups distilled water
- 1 cup chopped spinach leaves
- 10 pieces mint leaves
- 2 whole pitted dates
- 2 tablespoons raw cashew butter

Directions

1. Thoroughly wash the applicable fruits and vegetables.

2. Blend the spinach and water until smooth. Add everything else and blend until smooth.

3. Serve.

Cucumber Avocado Lime (15)

Stevia is a calorie-free super-sweetener that is made from a plant.

Serves 1.

Ingredients

- 1 cup spinach leaves
- ¼ cup water
- 3 limes, peeled and quartered
- ½ cup sliced cucumber
- ½ avocado, peeled
- Sweetener (honey, agave or stevia) to taste
- 4 ice cubes

Directions

1. Thoroughly wash the applicable fruits and vegetables.

2. Blend the spinach, limes and water until smooth. Add everything else and blend until smooth.

3. Serve.

Spinach Oats Vanilla (15)

This smoothie doesn't contain any fruit, depending upon the coconut milk and the vanilla extract for much of its flavor.

Serves 1.

Ingredients

- 1 cup spinach leaves
- 1 ½ cups water
- ½ teaspoon vanilla extract
- Pinch of salt
- ¼ cup unsweetened coconut milk
- ½ cup oats
- ½ cup ice cubes

Directions

1. Thoroughly wash the applicable fruits and vegetables.

2. Blend the spinach and water until smooth. Add everything else and blend until smooth.

3. Serve.

Smoothies with Dairy Products

Dairy products have come under fire by many nutritionists because of some of the modern dairy practices, including the use of questionable hormones and antibiotics in the production of milk and other dairy products. But there are organic dairy products available in some areas. Raw milk is a nice option if you aren't lactose intolerant, and some homemade dairy products can be quite healthful.

The recipes below call for dairy products, but you can easily substitute with non-dairy counterparts like almond milk, coconut milk, non-dairy yogurt and other non-dairy substitutes.

But real dairy products are hard to beat for the richness they provide in smoothies, and you might want to treat yourself occasionally. You also have a wide variety of dairy products to choose from, so you can substitute freely for the milk and yogurt in the recipes in this section.

Spinach Carrot Banana Yogurt (1)

For a real treat, you can substitute maple syrup for the honey in this recipe.

Serves 1.

Ingredients

- 2 cups baby spinach leaves
- 1 banana
- 1 carrot, peeled and cut into large chunks
- ¾ cup plain fat-free yogurt
- 2 tablespoons honey

- ¾ cup ice

Directions

1. Put all the ingredients into a blender and blend them until smooth.

2. Serve immediately.

Nutrition per Serving

- Calories: 388
- Carbs: 83 g
- Fat: 1 g
- Protein: 14 g
- Sodium: 221 mg
- Sugar: 64 g

Avocado Yogurt Milk (1)

Thick and creamy. Though avocadoes are technically fruits, they're more like a vegetable in many ways. For example, they're more commonly used in vegetable dishes like salsa than in fruit salads, so I'm considering avocadoes as a green in a few recipes.

Serves 2.

Ingredients

- 1 ripe avocado, halved and pitted
- 1 cup milk
- ½ cup vanilla yogurt
- 3 tablespoons honey
- 8 ice cubes

Directions

1. Put all the ingredients into a blender and blend them until smooth.

2. Serve.

Mango Avocado Yogurt (2)

Satisfy your sweet tooth with the sugar in this recipe, or opt to leave the sugar out.

Serves 1.

Ingredients

- ¼ cup mango cubes
- ¼ cup mashed ripe avocado
- ½ cup mango juice
- ¼ cup fat-free vanilla yogurt
- 1 tablespoon freshly squeezed lime juice
- 1 tablespoon sugar
- 6 ice cubes

Directions

1. Put all the ingredients into a blender and blend them until smooth.

2. Optionally garnish with sliced mango or strawberry.

3. Serve.

Spinach Pear Avocado Yogurt (4)

This yummy smoothie hits the spot.

Serves 1.

Ingredients

- 6 ounces plain nonfat Greek yogurt
- 2 cups spinach leaves, packed
- 1 ripe pear; peeled, cored and chopped
- 15 green or red grapes
- 2 tablespoons chopped avocado
- 2 tablespoons freshly squeezed lime juice

Directions

1. Blend the yogurt and spinach in a blender until smooth. Add the rest of the ingredients and blend them until smooth.

2. Serve.

Beet Berries Yogurt (5)

As a change of pace, we're substituting a red for a green here, as we use beets instead of a traditional green vegetable.

Serves 1.

Ingredients

- 1 cup fresh blueberries
- ½ cup fresh or frozen raspberries
- 1/3 cup cooked beet root, sliced
- ¼ cup nonfat Greek yogurt
- ¼ cup fresh orange juice
- 1 teaspoon light agave nectar

Directions

1. Put all the ingredients into a blender and blend them until smooth.

2. Serve.

Spinach Honeydew Yogurt (5)

Under 200 calories in this mild-flavored drink.

Serves 1.

Ingredients

- 1 cup fresh baby spinach leaves
- 1/3 cup nonfat vanilla Greek yogurt
- 1 ½ cups chopped fresh honeydew melon

Directions

1. Blend the spinach and yogurt in a blender until smooth. Add the melon and blend them until smooth.

2. Serve.

Kale Grape Oats (7)

A refreshing and light smoothie with a delicate aroma.

Serves 2.

Ingredients

- 1 cup kale leaves
- ½ cup crushed ice
- 2 kiwi fruits, peeled
- ¼ cup rolled oats
- 2 tablespoons honey
- 1 cup seedless green grapes
- 1 cup plain yogurt

Directions

1. Put all the ingredients into a blender and blend them until smooth.

2. Serve.

Green Monster (8)

Serves 1.

Ingredients

- 2 big handfuls spinach
- ¼ cup old-fashioned oats (uncooked)
- 1 banana (peeled and frozen)
- 1 tablespoon almond butter
- 1 cup skim milk
- 1 handful ice

Directions

1. Put all the ingredients into a blender and blend them until smooth.

2. Serve.

Blueberry Avocado Kefir (13)

Creamy and decadent.

Serves 1.

Ingredients

- 1 cup spinach
- ¾ cup water
- ¼ cup coconut kefir
- 4 ice cubes
- 1 cup blueberries
- ¼ avocado

Directions

1. Blend the spinach and water until smooth. Add everything else and blend until smooth.

2. Serve.

Spinach Yogurt Strawberries (15)

You can easily substitute other berries for the strawberries or use a mixed variety of berries.

Serves 2.

Ingredients

- 2 cups chopped spinach leaves
- 1 large whole orange
- ½ cup sliced bananas
- 1/3 cup strawberries
- 1/3 cup plain yogurt
- 1 cup ice cubes

Directions

1. Blend everything until smooth.

2. Serve.

Lime Banana Spinach (15)

You can substitute unsweetened non-dairy milk for the milk. You can also substitute a few strawberries or blueberries for the lime juice.

Serves 1.

Ingredients

- 2 cups shredded spinach leaves
- 1 cup milk
- 2 tablespoons lime juice
- 1 cup sliced ripe bananas
- ¼ teaspoon pure vanilla extract (alcohol-free)
- 1 tablespoon sunflower butter
- 1 whole pitted date

Directions

1. Blend the spinach and milk until smooth. Add everything else and blend until smooth.

2. Serve.

Yogurt Spinach Apricot (15)

You can substitute sugar-free soy yogurt for the non-dairy yogurt.

Serves 1.

Ingredients

- 1 cup spinach
- ½ cup non-dairy milk
- 3 small whole peaches
- 1 tablespoon sesame seeds
- ¼ cup dried apricots (pre-soaked for a smoother blend)
- ½ cup non-dairy yogurt
- ½ cup ice cubes

Directions

1. Blend the spinach and milk until smooth. Add everything else and blend until smooth.

2. Serve.

Blueberry Broccoli Banana (15)

You can add a ¼ cup of raisins or other dried fruit to increase the fiber and sweetness.

Serves 1.

Ingredients

- ½ cup broccoli, chopped
- ½ cup milk
- ½ cup water
- ½ cup blueberries
- ½ cup sliced bananas
- ½ cup oats
- 1 tablespoon sunflower seeds
- ½ cup ice cubes

Directions

1. Blend the broccoli, milk and water until smooth. Add everything else and blend until smooth.

2. Serve.

Muesli Romaine Dates (15)

Muesli is a granola-like breakfast dish consisting of raw rolled oats and various seeds, nuts and fruits. So in effect, this recipe contains a little of everything but the kitchen sink. You can certainly use this recipe for a filling and nutritionally complete breakfast.

Serves 1.

Ingredients

- ½ cup milk
- ½ cup water
- ½ cup romaine lettuce
- ½ cup ripe mango chunks
- ½ cup diced ripe bananas
- ½ cup muesli
- 1 tablespoon sesame seeds
- ¼ cup pitted dates

Directions

1. Blend the lettuce, milk and water until smooth. Add everything else and blend until smooth.

2. Serve.

Conclusion

Thanks again for downloading this book.

I hope the recipes in this book have inspired you to make smoothies, a simple and small step that can produce big results. Smoothies are among the healthiest of foods, providing a power-packed boost of energy that can enliven and enrich anyone's health and well-being.

This book has provided fifty quick and simple recipes for delicious smoothies that can help readers permanently shed even the stubbornest of pounds. The smoothies from these recipes were provided in a simple and consistent format that enabled readers to create nutritionally balanced smoothies that can serve as snacks or meals for people on the go. This book also provided the info necessary for creating your own smoothie recipes according to your specific needs and tastes.

I hope this book leads you to make smoothies as a real lifestyle change, setting you on a path that might lead you to a richer, healthier and happier life.

Helpful Resources

1. http://allrecipes.com/recipes/drinks/smoothies/

2. http://www.prevention.com/weight-loss/flat-belly-diet/smoothie-recipes-weight-loss

3. http://www.doctoroz.com/slideshow/9-slimming-smoothies?gallery=true

4. http://www.fitnessmagazine.com/recipes/drinks/healthy-choices/diet-smoothie-recipes/?page=2

5. http://www.cookinglight.com/eating-smart/smart-choices/low-calorie-smoothies

6. http://simplegreensmoothies.com/recipes

7. http://www.nutribulletrecipes.org/author/ali/

8. http://www.yummly.com/recipes/rolled-oats-smoothies

9. http://www.100daysofrealfood.com/2013/12/26/green-smoothie-recipe/

10. http://www.incrediblesmoothies.com/tag/weight-loss-recipe/

11. http://www.thebestofrawfood.com/green-smoothie-recipe-2.html

12. http://amrelnawawy.hubpages.com/hub/Green-Smoothie-Recipes-For-Weight-Loss-and-Healthier-Body

13. http://www.hayliepomroy.com/great-green-smoothies/

14. *Smoothie Recipes for Weight Loss* by Troy Adashun

15. *Green Smoothie Recipes for Weight Loss and Detox* by Jenny Allan

Preview of Gluten Free Diet Guide: A Blueprint to Jump Starting a Healthy, Low Budget, Gluten-Free Diet

Background

Gluten is a protein compound present in cereal grains such as wheat, rye and barley. Gluten is a Latin word which translates to "glue," referring to the combined water-insoluble proteins, gliadin and glutenin. Gluten is the substance that makes dough elastic and processed food items like bread, pasta and pastries chewy. This substance may also be present in cosmetics such as make-up and hair products.

A significant percentage of the population in North America have sensitivity to gluten where they experience an elevated immunologic response when they ingest foods that contain gluten. This usually leads to symptoms such as joint pain, anemia, tiredness, infertility, neurological disorders, dermatitis, and celiac disease, an autoimmune disorder.

The only known treatment for these health issues is to totally embrace a gluten-free diet. This means the person has to steer clear of foods that contain rye, barley, wheat, and other associated cereal grains. Because of the popularity of these grains in the food market, it is possible that items claiming to be gluten-free may have minute amounts of wheat, rye, or barley that is substantial enough to cause symptoms to persons that are sensitive to gluten.

Symptoms and disorders caused by gluten-containing food items

A review from the New England Journal of Medicine came up with a listing of illnesses caused by ingestion of gluten. Symptoms include Attention Deficit Hyperactivity Disorder (ADHD), anxiety, arthritis, depression, Irritable Bowel Syndrome (IBS), recurrent headaches, osteoporosis, eczema, fatigue, uncoordinated muscles, compromised immune system, inflammation of organs, excessive growth of fungus, weight loss or weight gain, and deficient nutrition. People who are hypersensitive to gluten are at high risk to develop diabetes, Gastro-Intestinal cancers, obesity, brain disorders, thyroid problems, and autism.

Costs involved with a gluten-free diet

A recent study assessed the economic burden of subscribing to a total gluten-free diet. The researchers conducted an analysis of food products that use wheat classified by brand name, size or weight of the package, and evaluated them in contrast to items that are gluten-free. The price disparities were also evaluated among different store venues like general stores, more expensive grocery stores, health food stores, and online grocery sites.

The study found that availability of gluten-free products varies among stores. General grocery stores offer 36 percent, while upper class grocery stores have 41 percent, and health food stores carry 94 percent in comparison to a hundred percent availability in online grocery sites. On the whole, all gluten-free products were costlier than wheat-based food items. Gluten-free pasta and bread are double the price of wheat-based pastas and breads.

Apparently, the purchase venue had more impact on the price ranges than geographic location. Researchers conclude that gluten-free items are not as available and are costlier than products that contain gluten. The author emphasizes that there is a need to address availability and cost issues of gluten-free foods that affect the dietary adherence and quality of life of gluten-sensitive consumers.

To fully enjoy this book, visit:

http://www.amazon.com/Gluten-Free-Diet-Guide-Blueprint-ebook/dp/B00I135OZO

Did You Like This Book?

Before you leave, I wanted to say thank you again for buying my book.

I know you could have picked from a number of different books on this topic, but you chose this one so I can't thank you enough for doing that and reading until the end.

I'd like to ask you a small favor.

If you enjoyed this book or feel that it has helped you in anyway, then could you please take a minute and post an honest review about it on Amazon?

Click here to post a review.

Your review will help get my book out there to more people and they'll be grateful, as will I.

More Books You Might Like

Household DIY: Save Time and Money with Do It Yourself Hints and Tips on Furniture, Clothes, Pests, Stains, Residues, Odors and More!

DIY Household Hacks: Save Time and Money with Do It Yourself Tips and Tricks for Cleaning Your House

Essential Oils: Essential Oils & Aromatherapy for Beginners: Proven Secrets to Weight Loss, Skin Care, Hair Care & Stress Relief Using Essential Oil Recipes

Apple Cider Vinegar for Beginners: An Apple Cider Vinegar Handbook with Proven Secrets to Natural Weight Loss, Optimum Health and Beautiful Skin

Body Butter Recipes: Proven Formula Secrets to Making All Natural Body Butters that Will Hydrate and Rejuvenate Your Skin

If the links do not work, for whatever reason, you can simply search for these titles on the Amazon website to find them.

CPSIA information can be obtained at www.ICGtesting.com
Printed in the USA
LVOW04s1949240615

443701LV00027B/1233/P